The Selfish Son Comes Home

Written by Lora Schrock

Illustrated by Isidre Mones

There once was a kind man who had two sons. The younger son was bored with living at home and asked his father for some money. Although his father thought it was a bad idea, he said yes.

"I'm going to the big city to find fun and excitement," the son said. "I may never go home again."

The son packed the money into a sack and left home. He didn't think about the family he was leaving.

His father sadly waved good-bye.

In the city, many people saw the son's money sack. They told him where he could buy the most expensive food and the finest clothes.

"The city is wonderful!" the son said. "I won't go home again!"

The son bought food and drink without thinking about saving his money.

He bought presents for all his new friends and threw many parties without thinking of his father.

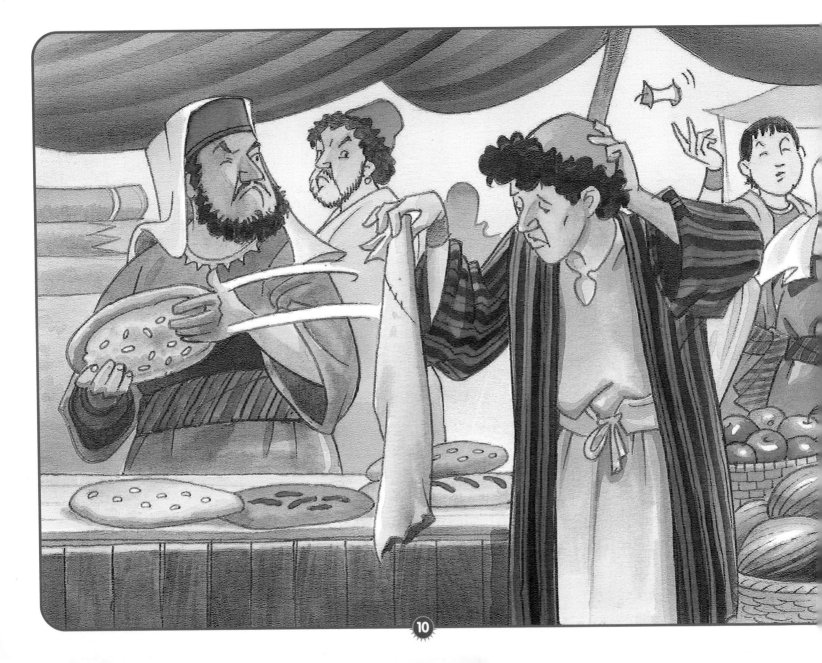

Soon the son's sack of money ran empty. His new friends left him all alone.

The son remembered his kind father and comfortable home.

"Should I go back?" he wondered. "I feel ashamed of the way I have lived. No, I can't go home again."

The son got a job in the country taking care of pigs. He was very poor and very lonely.

The son also was hungry. He was so hungry, he even wanted to eat the pigs' food. He began to cry.

"I've been so selfish!" he said. "I will tell my father that I am very sorry. Maybe I can go home again."

Taking his empty sack, the son left the pigs and began walking.

While he was still a long way from home, the son saw someone running toward him. Who could it be? He smelled like pigs and was very dirty. Who would want to rush out and greet him?

It was his father! The old man hugged and kissed his youngest son.

"I have done many foolish things," the son said. "I spent all my money and now it is gone. I am very sorry. I don't deserve to come home again."

His father called everyone over. "Tonight we will have a feast. My son was lost, but now we will celebrate because he has come home again."

Everyone cheered.

The Selfish Son Comes Home

Life Issue: I want my child to know that God is committed to us.

Spiritual Building Block: Commitment

Do the following activities to help your child understand that committed means "being in relationship through the good and the bad times":

Sight: Hide something special, such as a sticker or a cookie. Invite your child to look for the surprise, guiding him or her by saying *hot* when near and *cold* when far away. Later, talk with your child about how God is always seeking us. We are hidden when our hearts are turned away from him.

Sound: Ask your child how many months it is until his or her birthday. Help him or her figure it out. The kind father in this story always looked forward to his younger son's return. Ask your child to tell you what he or she looks forward to the most on her birthday.

Touch: Act out the ending of this story. First, you be the father and let your child be the son. Then switch roles. Remind your child that God always loves us and will always welcome us back, even when we do things that don't please him.

The Most Powerful King

Life Issue: I want my child to be humble in relationship to the Lord.

Spiritual Building Block: Humility

Do the following activities to help your child understand that to be humble is to "not be arrogant or proud":

👁 **Sight:** Watch a sporting event on television with your child, and note how the players act when they score a point or when the game. Do they act humble?

👂 **Sound:** Play some praise songs that emphasize God's greatness. Ask your child to sing along.

🤚 **Touch:** Have your child act out how he or she would act if a famous king or president came in the room. Would he bow? Would she curtsy? Explain to your child that he or she should act the same when in the Lord's presence.

The Brave Little Shepherd

Written by Lora Schrock

Illustrated by Joe Boddy

To Meghan

Faith Kidz® is an imprint of
Cook Communications Ministries, Colorado Springs, CO 80918
Cook Communications, Paris, Ontario
Kingsway Communications, Eastbourne, England

THE BRAVE LITTLE SHEPHERD
© 2006 by Cook Communications Ministries for text and illustrations

First Printing, 2006
Printed in India
1 2 3 4 5 6 7 8 9 10 Printing/Year 10 09 08 07 06

Cover: Sandy Flewelling
Interior Design: Sandy Flewelling
Interior Layout: Julie Brangers

ISBN: 0-7814-4470-5

The Brave Little Shepherd

Israel faced a war with the Philistines, who were led by a giant named Goliath. Goliath stood nine feet tall and wore shiny bronze armor.

The Israelites were afraid. How could they defeat this giant? To their surprise, a brave little shepherd named David said, "I will fight Goliath."

He didn't carry a spear or even a bow and arrow. He had only a slingshot.

When Goliath saw that David was just a boy, he let out a loud roar. "Can't you see that I am as tall as a tree? You can't beat me!"

But David didn't run away.

"Can't you see my shiny bronze armor?" Goliath shouted. "You can't beat me!"

But David didn't run away.

"You may have a sword," he said. "But I have the Lord. Today, he will help me beat you."

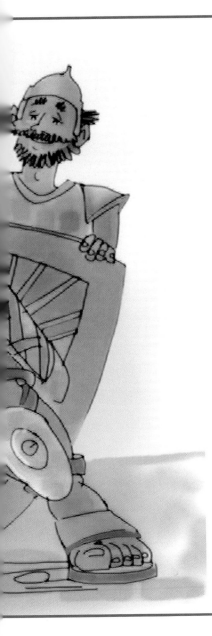

All the Philistines laughed. How could five smooth stones defeat the powerful Goliath?

Goliath was not afraid of David's five smooth stones or David's God. The giant pulled out his heavy, sharp sword and stepped forward.

But David didn't run away.

Instead, he put one of the smooth stones in his slingshot and began to swing it.

Faster and faster the slingshot spun. The faster it went, the angrier Goliath became.

But David didn't run away.

"When I beat you," David said, "everyone will know it was because of God."

Whoosh!

The stone flew from
David's slingshot.

The Israelites prayed.
Would they be saved?

Smack!

The stone struck Goliath on the forehead, and he fell to the ground. David had won!

When the Philistines saw Goliath wasn't getting up, they all ran away. Israel was saved!

"Goliath is defeated," David said. "And it is all because of God."

Faith Parenting Guide

Ages 4-7

Trust

The Brave Little Shepherd

Life Issue: I want my child to trust in God when facing tough times.

Spiritual Building Block: Trust

Do the following activities to help your child understand that trust means "belief in and reliance on the integrity, strength, ability, and surety of a person or thing."

Sight: For three nights in a row, show your child that the sun always sets in the west. Explain that he or she can always trust that God will do what he says he will, just like the sun always sets in the west.

Sound: Have your child tell you about a time someone he or she felt disappointed by a friend. Explain that while people can break your trust, God never will.

Touch: Have your child stand in front of you with his or her back toward you. On the count of three, have your child pretend to be a tree falling in the forest and fall back into your waiting arms.

The Most Powerful King

Written by Lora Schrock
Illustrated by Alastair Graham

King Nebuchadnezzar was very handsome. He wore the finest silk robes, and his dark hair was neatly combed. He walked through his kingdom proudly.

"Isn't my city wonderful? Isn't my palace grand? And it's all because I am the most powerful king that ever was. No one is greater than I am."

Suddenly a voice boomed from the heavens. "You are not the most powerful king—the Lord is! You are not greater than he is. Until you admit that is true, you will lose your kingdom."

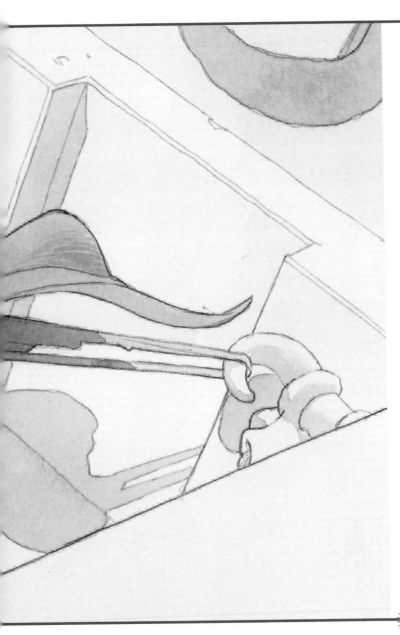

The king was frightened. Suddenly, he no longer had control over his city or his palace, so he ran away.

Far from home, the king wandered. Brambly bushes and thorny thorns tore his silk robes.

The voice called out again. "Until you admit that God is the most powerful king, you will live like a wild animal and eat grass for dinner."

The king fell to his knees and ate grass for dinner.

The voice called down a third time.
"Until you admit that God is the most
powerful king, your hair will grow
like feathers."

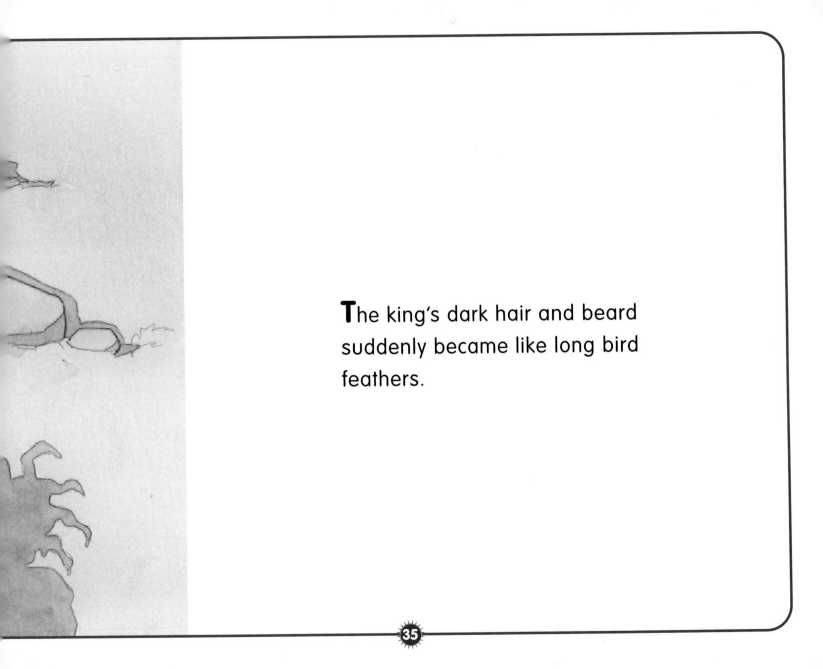

The king's dark hair and beard suddenly became like long bird feathers.

King Nebuchadnezzar had learned his lesson. He looked toward heaven.

"The Lord is the most powerful king ever," the king said. "Everything he does is right and just."

All at once, God restored the king's clothes, hair, and kingdom to him. Because Nebuchadnezzar was now humble and gave God the glory for everything, the Lord made him a great king among men.